EXCLUDING RITA

A psychoanalytic perspective on society's
dysfunctional response to challenging behaviour
of school pupils

If we, as the teaching profession, can rise to the
challenge of these insights, we will no longer
continue to further abuse damaged children. We
won't be aloofly delivering a curriculum to an
address where they cannot live. We will be
teaching effectively. We will see young people
begin to be more in control of their less
conflictive, emerging selves. We will see them
beginning to own their acquisition of learning,
skills, and sensibilities.

To

Glynis Eley

Exemplar extraordinaire of the art of caring
teaching

With grateful thanks to Chadha Degachi for her IT skills

In the beginning God gave to
every people a cup of clay
And from this cup they drank
their life.

Proverb of Digger Indians
Quoted, Ruth Benedict

CHAPTER ONE

BREAKING RITA IN

Insights and techniques from the phenomenology of psychoanalytic practice [1] have effectively been ignored in mainstream British schools for the best part of 100 years. There is an absence of much of these insights from British but not European initial teacher trainings. I shall argue that the absence of such insights has by default permitted some of the most vulnerable in society to be excluded as deviant and to be denied access to an appropriate education that has been their legal right for at least 50 years.

---

[1] For use of this term see later reference to David Armstrong in chapter 3.

The resistance to the introduction of this material is very complex. I believe that amongst the reasons is resistance to the requirement to conceive of the teacher-pupil *relationship* as just that. A demand that the teacher and his managers face up to their personal 'inadequacies' not as teachers but as people relating to pupils as individual young people. This involves recasting the perception of the power structure of the relationship. A start would be to see the pupil as the fee-paying client that she actually is. This would make the system downward referencing to the needs of the pupil not as it is now, overwhelmingly upward referencing to the demands of the educational system as an instrument of a politically driven society's economic goals.

But I would want to go further than that. I want the relationship to be conceived of in affective personal terms because thereby I would sensitise the teacher to the affective content of her classroom relationships and its influence upon her own *unconscious* processes. I speak of 'inadequacies' because there is a simple lack of training that would enable the teacher to conceptualise her *conscious*, so often negative, affective experiences in her workplace and thereby make them intelligible to and accessible from her professional role in *loco parentis* whilst maintaining her 'enabling' as distinctly different from inappropriate attachment.

I shall suggest it is also highly desirable that teachers understand the *unconscious* social phenomena that shape the life of the school as an organisation. Unconscious social phenomena powerfully influence the careers of both staff and pupils as the teacher responds to the group as group and to individuals as members of a group whilst they are themselves being inextricably influenced by unconscious group processes. To reach this understanding is not only intellectually demanding, it is emotionally demanding. Writing of a different organisational context, David Armstrong says:

> I think that what I am trying to share can be seen as a bringing into view at an organisational level of something known in the organisation, known in the emotional and physical and perhaps imaginal life of the organisation, which has resisted formulation: something primary and ordinary, that is lived, but only as a shadow. And once formulated, once brought towards thought, paradoxically creates a difference which makes a difference to how every decision, policy, action is understood. It does not

make things any easier; it does not show a client what to do. But it discloses meaning: introduces the client, as it were, to the organisation-in-himself and himself-in-the-organisation. And this disclosure sets a new agenda. [2]

I shall expand upon these ideas[3] but I am going to propose that the use of such insights has such obvious advantages that they will resonate with the everyday experience of every teacher and education manager. Such research as there is, points to significant benefits both to pupils and to practitioners of such awareness.

---

[2] David Armstrong, *Group Relations: Making absences present: The contribution of W.R. Bion to understanding unconscious social phenomenon*, (www.human-nature.com, 1998)

[3] See chapter 3.

I am going to propose also that there are pressures mounting inside schools and the wider society from disaffected adolescents that are providing both the urgent need and the opportunity for this lack to be addressed. Recognising and meeting the needs of the disaffected will benefit the wider school community not just by minimising disruption but by informing the entire educational process. Inadvertently the present government has created the opportunity.

The disruptive classroom behaviour of many adolescents in the nation's schools is currently the focus of much attention. There is a rise in the number of such pupils being permanently excluded from school. This may not be because such behaviour is necessarily on the increase; it may be because a changing managerial climate in the schools has reason to be less tolerant of such behaviour.

Under the 1944 Education Act, schools in England and Wales, have the legal duty to provide an education that is appropriate to the age, ability and aptitude of the pupils in their care. Since the adoption of the revised National Curriculum in 1997 the core of that provision has been closely defined by central government. The aggressive leadership by Chris Woodhead then of the Office for Standards in Education has by means of external inspection of classroom teaching brought tremendous pressure upon Schoolteachers and their managers. In a speech to the National Association of Head Teachers in June 1999, the first by a serving Prime Minister, Tony Blair asserted his determination to implement his policy of payment by results despite their opposition. He went on to announce that he had given a contract to an American management consultancy to devise the implementation of the policy.

It may be that these external pressures are in part responsible for the rise in exclusions from schools of disaffected pupils. From 1992 to 1998 the rise was in the range 25-30% year on year in Kent.[4] There are trends that disruptive behaviours previously associated with adolescent boys are increasingly being presented in Primary Schools and amongst Secondary age girls. Feminists might comment that as females take a less repressed role in society, including the society of the school, it is to be expected that they might be seen to be

---

[4] From September 1997 to July 1999 I have been visiting and working in mainstream and special schools in Kent. My present focus upon Kent is because the contemporary nature of my experience gives a useful context in which to understand the implications of national policy and practice.

exhibiting behaviours previously mainly associated with males.

Exclusions amongst primary age children were on the rise, 1992 to 1998. [5] In the educational year beginning September 1999, for the first time, in West Kent alone, provision was having to be made for seven, 'unmanageable' five year olds to be accommodated in a Pupil Referral Unit rather than progressing normally from Nursery Classes to Reception Classes. These Pupil Referral Units or PRUs educate pupils who have been excluded from mainstream state schools on the grounds of disruptive behaviour. Typically they will have 6-8 pupils in a class with at least one teacher and two learning support assistants

---

[5] Personal communication from a Kent County Council, Exclusions Officer.

Under the new pressure to be seen to be effectively, meaning measurably, delivering the curriculum, it would be understandable if teachers were less tolerant of behaviour that affected their performance or that of their pupils. Faced with being named and shamed as the manager of a failing school it would not be surprising if Heads followed the much lauded example of the incoming Head of an infamous rioting West Riding School and permanently excluded 'the ringleaders.'

The government response to the rise in permanent exclusions has been to put in place measures that influence the schools to solve the problem of disaffection within the school rather than exclude the pupil. These include obvious measures such as removing the funding for a pupil from the date of exclusion rather than permitting the funding to run for the academic year. With schools as budget holders this is a potent form of persuasion as budgets are very tight and each pupil is worth, depending upon key stage, around £2000+ per annum. More controversial is the institution of a sub committee of the governing body upon which the Headmaster may not sit and to which the pupil and his parents may appeal. This committee must endorse each permanent exclusion.

A new pressure upon the Local Authority will be that from September 1st 2002 excluded pupils must receive a full time education if educated other than at school. This will mean a huge increase in the provision of home tutors as the hours of tuition of such pupils jumps from the present three to four hours a week to twenty-five. Otherwise it will mean a major expansion of provision such as in the Pupil Referral Units that accommodate pupils deemed too disruptive for normal schools. Both these solutions are much more expensive than normal school places. They have been conspicuously unsuccessful in achieving results as measured by success at GCSE for the pupils themselves no matter how much it might have benefited the classes from which they were excluded.[6] It is obvious that Head Teachers will be under pressure from local authorities to come up with in-school solutions. This is the government's declared objective in its policy of inclusion.[7]

After 1997, there were important proposals that supported my central thesis of how these vulnerable pupils may be best supported in school. There was the requirement that before permanent exclusion, the school must be able to show that the pupil has

---

[6] DfEE, *Secondary School Performance Tables -1998.*
London, 1999.
[7] DfEE, *Social Inclusion: Pupil Support.* London, 1999.

received a concerted programme of pastoral support for the preceding four months and that s/he had not responded. Additionally because most exclusions occur in key stage four, there was a requirement that at least key stage three pupils be audited to alert the school to the needs of pupils with potential problems and ideally down to preschool nursery groups through Head Start programmes.

Nonetheless, in my view, despite those then welcome developments, there has not been an adequate DfEE formulation of the fundamental causes of these presenting behaviours. There has not been an appropriate DfEE formulation of solutions or provision of extra resources for the delivery of the pastoral support that it is required should be delivered to problem pupils or to the identified potential problem pupil, pupil with problems, families with problems.

And now, by 2012, such progress as there was is largely being thrown into reverse by the present government's return to facilitating exclusion by obviating the Head Teacher's legal requirement to justify his decision to a supervisory committee of school governors where previously he had had to set out the programme of support that he had provided..

I believe that currently pupil disaffection is being seen as an expensive problem for society and that it is the cost to society of these symptoms that is driving such government intervention as there is not a pastoral concern for the vulnerable individual pupil.

This 'concern' is being expertly presented as a fine sounding socially democratic concept of the right to inclusion in society. The cost to the individual of exclusion from education is being seen as social exclusion in the sense of exclusion from opportunities to live a normal economically productive life. An inclusive society is being defined as a society in which being in full employment and fulfilling ones duty to society by such employment and paying ones taxes is a just society in action. It must not be forgotten that these curricula and regulations are coming from a department for education and *employment*. They could just as well be coming from a department of education *for* employment.

This orientation is important for my theme because it tends to place conformity to the needs of society above the needs of the individual. This has resulted in an emphasis upon strategies for the management of behaviour that demand of the pupil a required level of conformity rather than an investigation of the causes of the behaviours. In practical terms the pupil is confronted with his failings and given a list of conforming behaviours to achieve. When he fails, he is presented with the evidence that he knew what was required, did not produce and therefore has earned his exclusion. Q.E.D. But what has changed in the behaviour of his teachers, the organisation of the school, his access to the curriculum, the relationship between his (usually separated) mother and father, his relationship to them, his socio-economic background, the anti-school subculture of his peer group or even in his own development. Usually nothing. So where is the change in his behaviour going to come from? In any other field of human endeavour to do something exactly the same but to expect different results would be regarded as irrational. In my view this kind of expectation takes place because of the special kind of school – pupil relationship. It is about a power relationship in which essentially the pupil has no power or advocacy except the 'advocacy' of disruption. It is my contention that it is the power relationships within education that determine which strategies are adopted not the efficacy of the strategies per se.

Writing in 1932, H.G. Wells expressed these assumptions thus:

The Community breaks in the individual by education, and sometimes that education involves disciplines of some severity. Education passes by insensible degrees into the public control of conduct, into the infliction of restraints, pains and penalties. There is no gap, no real dividing line between education proper and the prevention and punishment of crime; they are two aspects of the same thing.[8]

When in the last days of 20th century, researching as a student in a 'new' University whilst simultaneously an *officer* of an Education *Authority* yet a daily confidant of troubled children it was hard to disagree with how they felt or H.G.Wells wrote.

H.G. Wells. The Work, Wealth and Happiness of Mankind London Heinemann 1932 p.782

CHAPTER TWO

TRAINING RITA'S TEACHERS

The education of teachers to qualify to work in the British State system is regarded as a professional training and is undertaken in Institutes of Education within universities or what were called Training Colleges, then Colleges of Education often affiliated to Universities. The typical first qualification is now a three or four year specialist education degree or a post-graduate certificate in education following upon a degree in an academic subject or subjects. This training now takes place within Universities or in Colleges that have university status by affiliation. Teaching has becomes a graduate profession. The training includes a greater or lesser amount of time spent in classrooms in State schools actually teaching under supervision. The first year of employment as a teacher is regarded as an extension of training in that it is carried out under school and local authority supervision before the qualification is ratified and qualified teacher status is conferred.

An element of the curriculum of the trainee teacher is the psychology of education. In addition to the psychology of learning this course covers developmental psychology which has tended to be much influenced by Piaget and Tanner and their heirs. It is very unusual for British teachers to be required to read psychoanalytic texts that would give a psychoanalytic perspective on organisational, group and interpersonal behaviour.

It is interesting that this is so because European teacher trainings do include such reading. The British armed forces, industry and mental health services also have also made great use of the research that has followed upon the work of Bion and Foulkes at Northfields and later respectively at the Tavistock Clinic, and the Maudsley/Group Analytic Society.

Perhaps the early controversy in psychoanalysis that it should only be practised by the medically trained has been influential. This was strongly resisted by Freud and Ferenczi especially in the specific case of Rank a brilliant but non-medical protégé of Freud. Early prosecutions of non-medically qualified practitioners did take place in France and the unsuccessful fight to exclude non-medically trained psychoanalysts in the US was particularly bitter.

Although it was not the ostensible reason for their respective arrivals, perhaps because they would not then have been permitted to practice in the US, both Melanie Klein and later Anna Freud established themselves in Britain. Together they were the founding influences on child psychotherapy – despite their acrimonious personal and conceptual conflicts. It is known that Klein regretted abandoning her medical studies and made sure her daughter, Melitta received one. For a time Klein lived with a close friend and colleague, Susan Isaacs, a British educator and psychotherapist of some intellectual standing who ran a school and for some time taught at the London Institute of Education. Likewise Anna Freud had been a schoolteacher and her model of child psychoanalysis ascribes much importance to understanding a normal model of development from which neurotic behaviour is understood as a deviation.

As early as1908 Ferenzci wrote a vitally important paper on the implications of psychoanalysis for education:

A close study of Freud's work together with psychoanalyses conducted by ourselves, teaches us that faulty education is not only the source of faulty character development, but is also the source of serious illness; moreover we find that present day education is literally a forcing house for various neuroses.[9]

Here he is juxtaposing education and mental health and proclaiming loudly that they are often in opposition to each other. Too often, ninety years

---

[9] 'Psychoanalysis and Education' read at the First Psycho-Analytical Congress in Salzburg, 1908 reproduced in the 'International Journal of Psychoanalysis', 30 (1949), 220-224. Tran. by Michael Balint with 2 variants.

later, we assume that formal education is a good thing, perhaps because many parents see it as the royal road to a security and quality of employment superior to that which they themselves enjoy. It was a vote hungry politician that linked education and employment in a single ministry. But may not the focus of that juxtaposition tempt us to overlook the evils that Ferenczi identified as we justify the means by the desired ends?

Ferenzci does not deny the benefits of education but he is highly critical of methods and theories that are in 'In ignorance of the true psychology of man,' because, 'disregard for it in the course of education today create in social life numerous pathological phenomena.' The most obvious of these for him was ' that most people are almost wholly unable to find unselfconscious pleasure in the natural joys of life.'

However he also saw more sinister outcomes. He claimed that pupils, 'endured much unnecessary mental pain and suffering' because of inappropriate pedagogical methods and theories that induced damaging levels of repression. He spelled out the dangers of repression quite unequivocally:

What is repression? Perhaps it could best be described as a denial of facts. ...... Present day education has set out to achieve that man should cheat himself in disowning thoughts and feelings stirring within him. Psychoanalysis teaches that thoughts and impulses thus repressed from consciousness are by no means annihilated, but remain stored in the unconscious, and organise themselves into a dangerous complex of instincts, anti social and dangerous to the self.

It would be entirely inaccurate to suggest that the primary school classroom of the 19th Century and that of today can be sensibly compared but it is true to say that most teachers could not articulate the psychoanalytic principles that underpinned the move to a more liberal educational regime. It is not surprising therefore that the profession seems dangerously unaware of where current trends are leading. Unaware of the psychological dangers necessarily inherent in permitting the Chief Inspector of Schools, Chris Woodhead to decry the contribution of John Dewey to child centred education and to lead us by government mandate back towards a pedagogic model closer to that of Dickens's Mr Gradgrind who wanted to beat a boy raised in a circus for not understanding that a horse was a gramnivorous quadruped.

In the Secondary System, the vulnerable child, barely turned 11 years, is catapulted from a group of perhaps 30 children often maternally led by a teacher whom he has known for several years into as many as 15 different teaching groups. A bewildering range of personalities leads those groups with differing teaching styles and requirements of conformity. The groups themselves change year on year.

Freud concluded that the defining characteristics of the crowd are, 'invincibility, irresponsibility, impetuosity, contagion, changeability, suggestibility, collective hallucination and intellectual inferiority'.[10]

It would be fair to acknowledge that management of the modern secondary school are right to live in fear of these characteristics emerging if their school were to descend into chaos. Highly publicised examples prove it can happen. But the consequent regimentation of vast impersonal cohorts relies heavily upon repressive strictures to control the size and variability of populations up to 2000 strong.

Economies of scale do not automatically translate into a nurturing environment. They need to be mediated by a vastly effective pastoral system but that system itself needs to be enlightened. The first and most important step towards a better future lies – in my opinion – in the propagation of the knowledge of the true psychology of the child as

[10] Freud, S. *Group Psychology and the Analysis of the Ego* (London, Hogarth Press, 1959)

discovered by Freud. This last sentence is Ferenczi's. So why did it not happen?

He is known to have strongly influenced Melanie Klein whom he psychoanalysed and to whom it is suggested he proposed the play technique used in the analysis of children. His intimate relationship with the Freud household is said to have resulted in Freud suggesting Ferenczi marries Anna. So theoretically through Klein and Anna Freud, Ferenczi's insights could have flowed powerfully into British teacher training but it did not happen.

Sadly not only education was the poorer. His brilliant but before their time insights into what we now call post traumatic stress syndrome had him administering therapy to shell shocked First World War soldiers in the Austro-Hungarian army. Across no-mans land the British were prescribing the firing squad for similar symptoms. Despite Wilfred Bion's 1940's brave efforts - he was sacked six weeks after trying to create a therapeutic community out of military psychiatric rehabilitation ward – the British soldier had to wait for the Gulf War to receive similar support and then perhaps only because of high profile American practice. This itself undoubtedly flowed from American society's response to the grievous experience of trauma inflicted on a generation of enlisted conscripts in Vietnam. It is believed that double the number of American conscripts killed in action in Vietnam went on as veterans to commit suicide in later civilian life.

Perhaps war, particularly the Second World War has played a double role. Hitler's persecution of the Jews and banning of Freud's books led to a

Diaspora of psychoanalysts and helped speed the spread of Freud's thinking and followers to the four corners of the globe. But in England it transferred male psychoanalysts into the armed services and gave them tasks on the selection of officers, repairing the damage of war neuroses and preparation for re-entering civilian life. It also absented them from other areas of research and personal attendance at the BPS at a critical time where the conflict between Klein and A. Freud came to a head in the controversial discussions.

After the war much focus in mental health medicine was upon reparation. Having proved its worth in wartime hospital settings, psychoanalysis became firmly medicalised and psychotherapy became deliverable through the new National Health Service.

Post-war British education grappled with the Butler Act and busily interpreted it as a brief to build separate schools and create separate educational cultures for the academic and the non-academic. I once worked in a Comprehensive School converted from what had been the Secondary Modern built to house Butler's non-academic. The walls were half height clad in brown lavatory tiles. A mile along the road was the ex grammar school built for Butler's academics. Its walls were clad in oak panelling.

High performing pupils were sifted like wheat from chaff using intelligence testing that had patently served the purposes of war time selection and validated themselves in victory. Poor performance in school was obviously down to measurable genetic differences in intelligence. Pupils wore uniform, were subjected to military style discipline often delivered by a cohort of recently de-mobbed, emergency trained teachers for whom such a model of education would be reassuringly familiar. Without any other consideration, against this background it might be understandable why to this day any mention of psychoanalysis in a British school's staff room raises an eyebrow if not defensive banter. But there is the other consideration - the strong resistance that the notion of the 'unconscious' meets throughout society. That the phenomenon of resistance itself is one of the tenets of psychoanalysis is lost in the plethora of ill informed responses to the notion of the Unconscious – usually rendered as the 'subconscious' in ill-informed media coverage.

Tied as it is to concepts of mental illness, and evoking the reflected fearful responses to such illness, perhaps psychoanalysis cannot get a fair hearing as a descriptor of normal development or good educational practice. In contrast, psychology, educational psychology and educational psychologists are well entrenched in education. Many teachers would take the view that psychology's contribution to classroom practice is largely unseen and therefore assumed to be unproven because few psychologists are actually permitted by their roles to effect change by working extensively one on one with pupils.

That psychoanalysis as psychotherapy should be under a medical delivery system probably has also negatively impacted the intellectual status of psychoanalysis. It could be argued that the pioneering use of psychoanalysis to alleviate somatic symptoms of a distressed psyche laid upon the discipline a requirement for explanations in terms of medical science from the start which are just not available. Making psychoanalysis the intellectual bedfellow of medicine is full of risk. Its value and effectiveness can be undervalued just because medical models do not fit. For example, validating psychotherapeutic method by medically modelled outcome research is nigh impossible. There are severe ethical and logistical constraints against the use of long-term control groups. But before that problem could be tackled there is the bigger challenge of adequately categorising presenting symptoms, reliably diagnosing conditions then prescribing and delivering standardised therapeutic treatments. Simply put, psychotherapy simply is not like that. Applying the normative models of psychiatry found in DSM has very limited value. And if we try to reduce it to that which we can measure, then we are probably measuring something else. There is the concomitant danger of measuring what is measurable but then making what is measurable important simply because it is measurable.

To this day, budget holding medical general practitioners must authorise the provision of and payment for, psychotherapy received by schoolchildren. If a pupil is so referred, the clinic will ask whoever is responsible for the school's pastoral system to fill out a lengthy questionnaire on the child. The request appears in a letter that threatens that delay in replying or failure to reply could result in the child not being seen. There is also a stricture that other teachers should not be informed that the child is so referred. This last allegedly to protect the child's right to privacy. The reason for the referral is not revealed neither is the receipt of the completed form acknowledged. Most importantly the school is not notified of the outcome of the intervention, its initiation or its termination. This results in grave risks to pupil and teachers alike. A current case of mine involves a pupil who overdosed on a bottle of her father's Diazepam and arrived in school in a confused state. Fortunately an alert member of staff spotted the condition, the child was stomach pumped in time and saved. It transpires that the Child and Adolescent Mental Health Service had been seeing the girl for depression but had not informed the school of her vulnerability.

Kent has not spent money adequately to deliver psychotherapy to its school populace. Even when this child was accepted on to a waiting list, it would have been six months before she was seen. It would have taken several months to get her onto that list.

I recently intervened in aid of a pupil about to be excluded from school as uncontrollable and violently abusive. In June 98 he had been referred as out of control. An appraisal for ADHD was proposed. I discovered that it had taken until March 99 for him to be seen by a clinical psychologist and so diagnosed. In July 99 he was waiting for his appointment with a psychiatrist to receive Ritalin. The appointment was booked for September 99! His parents were in despair because his behaviour was breaking up the family. Without the Ritalin to calm him down he would not have survived the term still less be ready to benefit from the next academic year. At this crucial interface between medicine and education, Kent is in disarray.

Here the medicalisation of psychotherapy has swept up its delivery into the exclusive secrecy that still shrouds so many medical procedures. It has to be recognised that the men in white have an attitude of elitism that fosters the cult of confidentiality. This attitude not only endangers pupils it also puts a tourniquet upon the flow of ideas and procedures from psychotherapy into education in a highly specific form that could significantly enlighten educational practice. A government initiative could have helped to remedy this when it published, 'Working together under the Children's Act, 1989.'[11] It was a guide to interagency practice.' To my

---

[11] Department of Health Education and Science. London, HMSO, 1991.

certain knowledge this has not been implemented in Kent in a way that effectively involves all key players in daily casework. In January 2000 new consortia will be formed, education district based. Monthly case conferences will be held to plan support for disruptive pupils referred by the schools. The panel will be composed of Educational Psychologists, Educational Welfare Officers, Behaviour Support Staff, Youth and Community Workers and Police Liaison. Missing are the Child and Adolescent Mental Health Service and the Social Workers. Given that most emotional and behavioural difficulties seem to begin within the psychodynamic of the family and certainly powerfully impact it, this seems strange – until one remembers the territoriality of Services. But given the enormous difficulty in achieving intervention from both these missing Services their non-inclusion – it is not exclusion – seems plainly negligent. Doubly so when all involved appear to lament the lack yet non has the political will or clout to drive change.

I have been looking at historical and organisational reasons for the absence of Ferenczi's, proposed ' propagation of the knowledge of the true psychology of the child,' into education. But another potent reason could be the nature of this 'knowledge' as knowledge. Like medicine, psychoanalytic theory is empirical but simplistic notions of 'observer' and the 'objectivity' of what is 'reported,' break down when confronted with the task of understanding what is 'observed' in the phenomenology of psychoanalysis. I shall return to the concepts of transference and countertransference in more detail but these two phenomena alone transform the observer into a participant observer in a critical way.

The very 'subjectivity' of the observer is in fact of the essence of psychoanalytic understanding and of the validity of its formulations. We cannot adequately investigate the heart of subjectivity which is the human psyche other than by a process which has been described as, 'a process of empathy, ... moving into the 'hermeneutic circle' in order to understand the 'horizon of meaning' the subject inhabits rather than looking for objective facts.[12]

This process invariably involves an encounter with the Unconscious and its processes to which, again, I shall return but it is essential to grasp in the words of Michel Foucault that psychoanalysis sets 'itself

---

[12] Parker, Ian, *Exegesis of Habermas* in *Psychoanalytic Culture: psychoanalytic discourse in Western society* (London: Sage, 1997), p.143.

the task of making the discourse of the unconscious speak through consciousness.'[13] The phenomenology of psychotherapy is the language in which the contents of the unconscious articulate themselves

John Bowlby tried bravely to bridge an apparent gap between psychotherapy and cognitive psychology. This bridge might reasonably have been seen as viable to cognitively based education theorists but I have seen little evidence of traffic. He attempted to use the model of cognitive information processing to extend an understanding of the unconscious process of resistance, which he called defensive exclusion. Of the lifting of resistance he went on to say, 'analytic therapies can be understood as procedures aimed at enabling a

[13] Michel Foucault, *The Order if Things* (New York: Random House, 1970), p.374.

person to accept for processing information that hitherto he has been excluding in the hope that the consequences of his doing so will be equally profound.'

Bowlby here speaks of helping someone to come to accept for processing information that he has been excluding. Earlier I quoted Ferenczi talking of ' a denial of facts' and warning of the resulting unconscious complexes as 'dangerous to the self. The critical significance of those processes, like so many in psychotherapy, has no real content until it is experienced within the phenomenology of the practice of psychotherapy. But undoubted though the truth of that statement is to a practising psychotherapist, the subjective ground of its validation has led to a charge of creating a mythology of the human psyche not a science.

Leaving aside popular misconceptions of the 'objectivity' of so called science, perhaps, as some have suggested, psychoanalytic theory is a myth. Of explanations, Wittgenstein said, " But isn't it an inexact explanation? Yes, why shouldn't we call it 'inexact'? Only let us understand what 'inexact' means. For it does not mean 'unusable'."[14] Practically speaking the important question is whether it is a useful myth and more useful than alternatives for delivering desired results. This is a hotly contested issue and one that it is not the purpose of this thesis to address. I do refer to the recent positive results reported in a large- scale survey by Roth and Fonagy and reported in of one of the latest and most extensive reviews of the

---

[14] Wittgenstein, L. *Philosophical Investigations (Oxford: Blackwell, 1953), p.88.*

literature in the article of Hoag and Burlingame (p.68)

My starting point is that the clinical efficacy of psychoanalytic practice is established and that had insights from psychoanalytic practice emerged as an educational tool for describing normal development, interpersonal relationships and relationships with the self, then it would have been offered a comfortable chair in the school staffroom. Perhaps a chair it has slid into disguised as cultural or even literary studies and maybe could in future, as I shall later propose, enter in aid of those to whom the new Citizenship curriculum is addressed

More immediately, I wish to demonstrate that the classroom teacher can and should find enormous help in understanding and managing the phenomena of classroom behaviours when viewed through psychoanalytic lenses. It is also highly likely, in my opinion, that such pertinent utility will, for the experienced teacher, validate psychoanalytic theory.

CHAPTER THREE

REGISTERING RITA'S RESPONSE

I am now going to describe some basic psychoanalytic phenomenology that could help teachers to understand what is happening in their classrooms when they are encountering or countering disruptive adolescent behaviours. I wish to assert an important distinction here between ideas from psychoanalytic studies and what I earlier described as phenomenology from psychoanalytic practice.

I am grateful to David Armstrong[15] of the Tavistock Consultancy for this helpful terminology. I wish to

---

[15] David Armstrong, *The Recovery of Meaning.* Paper prepared for the annual Symposium of the International Society for the Psychoanalytic Study of Organisations: 'Organisation 2000 : Psychoanalytic Perspectives,' New York, June 1996

use it to refer to what is *experienced* in a relationship, when to use a phrase from Bion, all the senses are used in common. When all one's antennae are sympathetically functioning. I first came across this notion as a student of English literature, in Keates' negative capability. The ability to register what is going on passively but sentiently.

One can apply this level of sensibility to what is going on psychodynamically when one is working with individuals, with a group or when one is working in an organisation. It is a capacity to allow what is happening or not happening to *register* upon one's sensibilities without acting or responding other than to allow the emotional experience to run.

In another context, David Armstrong says of Bion that,

He had a quality amounting to a sixth sense which was the capacity to register and attend to the quality of emotional experience he was aware of in himself: apprehension, boredom, irritation, pressure to do or say something, or not to do or say something, the feeling of being on the receiving end of powerful expectations or feelings from others: admiration, contempt, envy, hatred, curiosity, love etc.

I would add the equal sense to be so aware of what is going on not only in himself but also in those around him. It is an important part of my thesis that sensitive, experienced teachers will recognise these experiences. I also maintain that to utilise theories based upon them will not require an extensive psychoanalytic training. Teachers will not be trying to analyse their pupils but they will be better equipped to be aware of the tone and structure of the pedagogic relationships that they have established and to fulfil the demands that the pastoral content of their work places upon them.

Firstly, what model of the relationship between themselves, their area of study and their group has the teacher, perhaps inadvertently, constructed? Is it a didactic model whereby he instructs and the pupil learns by copying and regurgitating the teacher's notes? A vertical model in which the teacher as expert passes down from an intellectual rostrum, as it were, the fruits of his personal scholarship.

Or is it a co-operative model in which she and her students engage in a mutual encounter with the subject. A horizontal model in which, side by side, they look together outwards towards an area of study. There maybe an element of artifice here as the teacher seeks to inhabit the comprehension horizon of the pupil but I submit that is really only a form of adjustment also necessary in interpreting their subject to a given key stage audience in the vertical model, albeit attitudinally adjusted.

Or is it a combination model that takes elements of each depending upon the task in hand.

The teacher should be consciously aware of the style that he is adopting and examine where his preferences lie. If he must always dominate, control and confront when challenged, then perhaps he needs to examine his fear of losing control. Is it grounded in an assessment of realistically volatile situation or is it an expression of a deeper personal insecurity.

In both models the teacher is going to be subjected to *transference* and to experience *countertransference.*

In the vertical model, the teacher may experience transference as a form of misrecognition. The didactic role is essentially authoritarian. The male pupil who is having major problems in his relationship with, say his father, because of unresolved oedipal conflict – competition for his mother's love - may transfer onto the authoritarian male teacher the aggression that is repressed at home by fear of real violence, significant sanction or unconscious castration anxiety. He 'sees' his father in the classroom and attacks when feeling confronted or made to acknowledge subservience to authority.

Interestingly in a recent article Chris Woodhead lambasted the influence of John Dewey on education, claiming that his books should be banned from teacher training courses. John Dewey favoured a co-operative approach to learning strongly involving the pupils own interests. Chris Woodhead's model mediated through the National Curriculum is very much more, I teach, you learn! A return to chalk and talk seems prescribed. In fact that method is actually spelled out in the new numeracy programme. The phenomena of transference would suggest that this style might provoke more confrontation in the classroom with troubled adolescents.

How does the teacher react to aggression? His reflexive feeling response could be his *countertransference*. What does the pupil make him feel? Is it anger that prompts reciprocated verbal violence. He should examine those feelings. Have those emotions been projected into him or have they been aroused in him by their resonance to experiences in his own Unconscious. And to what end. Earlier, I quoted David Rapaport, 'the dynamics of psychic manifestations are unconscious.' It is highly likely that he will not be immediately consciously aware of the origins of the emotions but he will be aware of the emotions themselves. And he must beware. In some sense the emotions may not be his but introjected from his pupil and so often the response that the emotions prompt will not be appropriate to the educative ends the teacher is there to achieve. He might calmly ask the pupil why he is angry with him or why he needs him to be angry. Equally the teacher might want to ask the question of himself.

The answer might just be, 'Because I do!' Realistically on a bad day a teacher may just become angry with the pupil, shout at him and maybe apply a sanction. This is a 'normal' and a 'human' response. Pupils can some times learn that they do provoke anger and need to learn about reparation. However, the ability of the professional educator to rise above the personal response, to be so self-aware and in control of her emotions that all reactions are premeditated to a given educational end is a requirement of her professionalism. It is one to which we can aspire and realistically achieve only most of the time. It is however essential to register our response *all* of the time. To be aware that we have lost control and to seek to understand, for example what it was that made us so threatened.

It is important to recognise that a pupil can provoke anger or rejection in rather more subtle ways that out and out confrontation. A pupil with very low self-esteem might project into the teacher a response that confirms the pupil's low judgement of himself. If ever the teacher is experiencing very negative emotions about a pupil he needs to examine those feelings carefully. He needs to determine whether they reflect a considered judgement or whether they are of the moment and the product of *introjection* from the pupil where uncannily the pupil will make us share his feelings about himself. In extreme cases a pupil will behave in such a way as to bring wrath down upon him and so confirm his self-judgement.

In group work or in the horizontal model, the teacher may experience projected onto him what

Bion has identified as an assumption of dependence. The teacher in this model is trying to make the students responsible for their own learning. The group responds by waiting for the teacher to take the initiative. They want the teacher to lead and support. They are fearful of independence. There is often a huge *resistance* to the development of maturation or personal growth. Often the teacher may feel a very strong temptation to yield to this pressure to lead. In effect to give up the attempt to foster maturation. That is exactly what the group wants. It is an emotion they have projected into the teacher. Again the emotion should be examined and evaluated to assess whether the group has genuinely met an impasse or whether it is a powerful resistance to learning from experience. Often the best approach will be to let the group wrestle with their frustration until they articulate it when the teacher might invite them to interpret what they are feeling and ask them why they might need him to lead. Then to ask the group to where is it *they* want to be led.

The teacher and the group might be surprised to experience very strong feelings of attachment bordering upon affection or equally negative feeling about a member. The power of the feelings may be out of proportion to anything undertaken in the group. Here Bion would say that groups have the power to trigger primitive psychotic fears similar to those identified by Melanie Klein in the acute distress and violent tantrums of the frustrated infant. These responses however irrational or irrationally justified must be recognised as valid for those that experience them. They have to deal with them, so therefore must we.

With a group of highly disturbed youngsters a teacher may be constantly blocked from progressing the lesson because objects or provocations are flying around the room. The pupils are constantly and successfully provoking each other to respond in similarly negative ways. When challenged or counselled the individual pupil will respond with, 'Its only a bit of a laugh, Miss,' or the like. But usually something much deeper is going on which is what makes it so hard to control. It is widely recognised that children who have been emotionally abused or worse are carrying around a lot of anger that they cannot locate appropriately. This anger tends to free float which is to say that it attaches it self, often inappropriately, to situations and incidents.

This constant needling, however, seems to be much more vicious. It is important to notice that the cruelty we are observing here is not arbitrary. Could it be that the pupils are expelling the hurt to which they have been subjected by projecting it into a classmate? Whatever the cause the pupils are off task in a big way and this form of disruption can so grip a teaching group that some teachers find that group unteachable. Some colleagues seem to be able to so dominate the group that the behaviours are repressed but, likely as not, they will resurface elsewhere that day, usually in the following lesson or on the corridor following that lesson.

I am talking about vicious provocation here. To give an actual example. Alan, a 12-year-old boy is going the next day to help collect his sister, Ellen, from hospital. He is very happy about it and tells anyone who will listen. She has recovered from a serious condition and nearly died in the hospital. His mate, John, asks his friend in front of others in a loud voice, 'Do you masturbate over Ellen?' A fistfight ensues.

It transpires that John's father recently died and that the hospital could not help him.

When John was questioned about the incident he made no reference to his father and made no connection with Alan's anxiety and relief over his sister's recovery. It was just a bit of fun. At John's conscious level it was just that but an experienced psychotherapist might interpret that the will to hurt flowed from the rage that *his* father had died whereas his friend's sister was alive and well. Perhaps the vitality of the sister's survival resonates in the fertile seed of fantasised masturbation. I do not expect the teacher to interpret in this way only to be alert to the fact that cruelty amongst children is rarely arbitrary.

I have observed this viciousness of needling in highly disturbed children in a therapeutic community but I have also seen it in a bottom secondary school set where the pupils have been setted by capacity for disruption – a so called sink set. If we can talk about a continuum of behaviours, we are entering now the realm of the seriously emotionally disturbed pupils rather than the average child and I shall return to address this kind of challenge under a different heading. That is I shall return to these themes in the context of more direct interventions that are now being successfully introduced in other settings and which could usefully be deployed in our schools.

CHAPTER FOUR

CITIZEN RITA

A potent form of the present government's response to disaffection is to see it in terms of Citizenship or rather the lack of it. They seem to be saying that adolescent disaffection can be explained as a lack of education i.e. the absence from the curriculum, specifically the National Curriculum for England and Wales of lessons in Citizenship.

This has led to an advisory group on Education for Citizenship and the Teaching of Democracy in Schools – set up in November 1997 by David Blunkett, the Secretary of State for Education and Employment. His old tutor, Professor Bernard Crick, Emeritus Professor of Politics and Sociology at Birkbeck College, chaired the group. The group presented its final report to David Blunkett on 22nd September (DfEE, 1998). The group's Professional Officer, seconded from the DfEE, was David Kerr. Addressing the national conference of the National Foundation for Educational Research in October 98, David Kerr described the advisory group's concern and its response in the following terms:

... The decline in traditional forms of civic cohesion has been termed a 'democratic deficit'. But perhaps the most pressing factor is the worrying signs of alienation and cynicism among young people about public life and participation, leading to their possible disconnection and disengagement from it. These factors have led to calls from many different quarters for citizenship education to be made an explicit, rather than an implicit, part of the school curriculum.[16]

Whilst lamenting the lack of research upon, 'the outcomes of citizenship education programmes on pupil knowledge, attitudes and behaviour,' he goes on to applaud that this committee has proposed the putting in place of a national programme of education in citizenship with:

A ' *statutory entitlement*'.... established by setting out a framework of specific learning outcomes for each key stage, rather than detailed programmes of study. This means substituting for the present input and output model of the existing National Curriculum subjects an output model alone based on tightly defined learning outcomes.

---

[16] Kerr, David, Paper prepared for the NFER's Annual Conference on 6th October 1998,

These outcomes are identified as:

1. Social and moral responsibility.

2. Community involvement.

3. Political literacy.

Which are 'tightly defined' as:

Firstly, **social and moral responsibility**, *children learning from the very beginning self-confidence and socially and morally responsible behaviour both in and beyond the classroom, both towards those in authority and towards each other.*

Secondly, **community involvement,** *learning about and becoming helpfully involved in the life and concerns of their communities, including learning through community involvement and service to the community.*

Thirdly*, political literacy, *pupils learning about and how to make themselves effective in public life through knowledge, skills and values. [Bold italics, D.Kerr's]

Critically this document proposes moral and political prescriptions to proscribe behaviours to achieve what are actually psychodynamic outcomes. I.e. we *ought* or *must* respond to authority or each other in socially acceptable ways and by implication if we are taught that this is so, then it shall be so. But is that how we learn to relate to the inside and the outside of ourselves, to imposed authority and to each other, especially in turbulent adolescence when perhaps we are trying to cut free from the psychological umbilical of parental and societal control (authority). Without an investment in society how would we feel a perceived benefit in such social cohesion (conformity)?

Kerr does identify problems. He recognises that, 'We must constantly guard against the feeling of a lack of meaning, direction and control in people's lives leading to alienation and cynicism' but does not specifically tie it to, 'the involvement of pupils in the development of school rules and policies.'

Stressing the need for involvement he says, 'this is essentially an issue of *involvement*. Schools can only do so much. They could do more, and must be helped so to do. However, pupils' attitudes to active citizenship are influenced quite as much by many other factors as by schooling: by family, the immediate environment, the media and the example of those in public life.'

He asks, ' … how we can involve parents, governors, community representatives and support agencies in citizenship education in meaningful partnership with schools.'

Laudably he declares,

' This is an issue of *participation*. Surprisingly, behind all activities of governments and big corporations, the world is still composed of individual human beings,'

He goes on to conclude. ' The challenge here is two-fold. To understand our roles and responsibilities as individual citizens in a modern democratic society, but also to think about the consequences of our actions.'

But he does not address the much more fundamental and difficult challenge. To understand how and why individuals relate to other individuals as individuals, to other groups of individuals, to individuals in authority and to authority wielded by groups.

Bowlby and Ainsworth have much to say about *attachment* that might apply to the disaffected. They may be 'avoidants' who as infants were constantly denied physical contact by their mothers. Avoidants tend to express behaviour of detaching themselves emotionally from their surroundings. It is hypothesised that this enables them to hide their vulnerability. [17]

Ainsworth's findings on socialisation in infants might also be apposite:

> Infants have a natural behavioural disposition to comply with the wishes of the principal attachment figure. This disposition

---

[17] J. Bowlby and M.D. Ainsworth, 'An Ethological Approach to Personality Development,' *American Psychologist*, 46, (1991), pp. 333-341.

emerges most clearly if the attachment figure is sensitively responsive to infant signals whereas efforts to train and discipline infants, instead of fostering the wished for compliance, tend to work against it.[18]

Bion declared that groups were fantasies but ones in which the individual invested meaning because a conglomeration of individuals have the power to re-awaken the infantile psychotic fears reported by Melanie Klein. Bion also reported the phenomenon in groups of a basic assumption of dependence in which responsibility for outcomes are projected on to the perceived leader and devolved from the self.

---

[18] M. D. Ainsworth, S. M. Bell, and D. J. Stayton, *Infant – mother attachment and social development,* in M. J. Richards (Ed), The integration of the child into a social world. (London: Cambridge University Press 1974. pp. 99-135.

Is not disaffection exactly that? These adolescents do not *feel* an identity with the interests of the school or its output nor often with their parents or a notional wider society. Is it too simplistic to ask what role affection can play in disaffection? Telling adolescents that they should feel involved or making explicit the consequences if they do not seems to have little penetration with this disaffected target group. It is tempting to predict that such a group will be as disruptive in a Citizenship class as in any other.

Is this empathetic feeling a skill to be acquired cognitively through a linguistically mediated belief system or is it an attitude brought about by an emotion and only later registered linguistically as a belief? Psychoanalysis asserts the centrality of *affect* but also the impenetrability of its springs within the Unconscious.

The essential basis of our personality is affectivity. Thought and action are only, as it were, symptoms of affectivity.[19]

Affects and emotions correspond with processes of discharge, the final expression of which is perceived as feeling.[20]

We take here as our basis a quite definite assumption as to the nature of the development of affect. This is regarded as a motor or secretory function, the key to the

[19] Carl Jung, *Uber die Psychologie der Dementia Praecox* (Halle: 1907), Quoted J. Hillman, Emotion, (Chicago: North Western University Press, 1961), p59.
[20] S. Freud, *The Interpretation of Dreams*, trans. A. A. Brill, (New York Modern Library, 1938), p.111.

innervation of which is to be found in the ideas of the Unconscious.[21]

In the final analysis the dynamics of psychic manifestations are unconscious, and cannot be found by investigating interrelations of the data of physiology and the data of consciousness.[22]

Which does not mean that the attempt is not made. Bowlby's theory of Defensive Exclusion postulates, that 'calls for attachment are defensively excluded because it leads a child's attachment behaviour and feelings to be aroused intensely but to remain unassuaged.'[23]

---

[21] S. Freud, *The Interpretation of Dreams*, trans. A. A. Brill, (New York Modern Library, 1938,) p.548
[22] D. Rapaport, *Emotions and Memory*, (International University Press, 1950), p.28.
[23] J. Bowlby, *Attachment and Loss*, Vol. iii. (London. Hogarth, 1980), p.73.

Lord Phillips, Chairman of the Citizen Foundation, introduced the debate in the House of Lords on the recommendations of the Crick Advisory Group on Education for Citizenship. Sadly, in his, the Government's official response to Crick, the formula had become, 'in order to contribute, young people need knowledge, skill and the *will*.'

Here he is reducing disaffection to conscious choice in a tone that resonates eerily of the magistrate's court.[24]

It would seem to me that a committee composed as it was of politicians, political theorists, administrators of educational, parole and prison organisations was ill fitted to address the fundamentals of these issues. Professionally they are tasked by society to manage the disaffected but

---

[24] 18 Jan 99, House of Lords.

they do so by defining disaffection as deviance and then by extension as antisocial even criminal. It seems that such a committee that appears to have had no one under thirty years of age and no sociologists, anthropologists or psychiatrists, is not one that would be sympathetic to the notion that deviance is socially defined thereby promoting secondary disaffection; that the convenient social label of deviance 'justifies' punitive sanctions in the popular mindset but it does nothing to make disaffection more intelligible or eradicable.

A social psychologist could have reminded them of Basil Bernstein's theory of educational transmissions. 'The 'expressive order' attempts to transmit an image of conduct, character and manner and tends to bind the whole school together as a distinct moral collectivity.' The 'instrumental order,' how the curriculum drives the acquisition of specific skills, may through academic segregation by ability and rank ordering of results, be divisive in function. Writing in 1975, he could be describing the educational scene 25 years later:

The more the instrumental order dominates schools in England, the more examination minded they become and the more divisive becomes their social organisation. The greater the emphasis on this type of instrumental order, the more difficult it is for the expressive order to bind and link all the pupils in a cohesive way.[25]

An anthropologist such as Ruth Benedict could have commented that very high prices are paid in terms

[25] Basil Bernstein, *Class Codes and Control*: Volume 3. Towards a Theory of Educational Transmissions. (London: RKP, 1975), pp. 44/5.

of human suffering and frustration when one generation creates normalities for the next. That adaptation to such 'normalities' can be better handled if they are seen as convenient arrangements not categorical moral imperatives deviation from which incurs such painful alienation. . She could also have said:

> The therapeutic problem of dealing with our 'psychopaths' of this type is often misunderstood. Their alienation from the actual world can often be more intelligently handled than by insisting that they adopt the modes that are alien to them. ... The misfit individual may cultivate a greater objective interest in his own preferences and learn how to manage with greater equanimity his deviation from the type. If he learns to recognise the extent to which his suffering

has been due to his lack of support in a traditional ethos, he may gradually educate himself to accept his degree of difference with less suffering. ... He may gradually achieve a more independent and less tortured attitude towards his deviations and upon this attitude he may be able to build an adequately functioning existence.

Tellingly she would also have observed that, 'an increased tolerance in society towards its less usual types must keep pace with the self education of the patient'. Asked, 'Who is the patient?' She would have answered, 'Tradition is as neurotic as any patient; its overgrown fear of deviation from fortuitous standards conforms to all the usual definitions of the psychopathic.'[26]

[26] Ruth Benedict, Patterns of Culture. (London, RKP, 1935), p.196.

A psychiatrist could have wondered aloud if by, disaffected, the politicians had identified a characteristic set of personality features composing the DSM 111-R descriptive criteria for a diagnosis of Borderline Personality Disorder. Viz.

Intense but unstable personal relationships; self destructiveness; constant efforts to avoid real or imagined abandonment; chronic dysphoria such as anger or boredom; transient psychotic episodes or cognitive distortions; impulsivity; poor social adaptation and identity disturbance.

He would have wondered how they intended to advise schools to manage BPD given that it poses considerable therapeutic and management difficulties to psychiatrists – even if one could get a pupil to see a psychiatrist in less than 6 months.[27]

I assert that these kinds of inputs from the human sciences are essential if Education is going to be managed centrally by politicians, which increasingly seems to be the intent. But even if they will not look outside of their own education, should we not challenge them within their own terms of reference.

Should we not be uneasy that it has long been the craft of politicians to marshal individuals into groups, to assert a commonality of interest and to instigate action, often, violent action, to achieve group aims – often the aims or agendas of the political classes. To call this agenda, Citizenship,

---

[27] Predicted waiting time, West Kent Child and Adolescent Mental Health Service.

seems to me to be begging a lot of questions that it is the role of a political education to raise. Why is non-engagement not seen as a valid form of criticism? Who has the right to say that it is the duty of young people to support a status quo that they might perceive as discredited? The Tabloids of the 1990s may be labelled the gutter press unfairly but they seem to have found an awful lot of prominent contemporary politicians crawling there.

I am not persuaded that any political party, even one wearing the mantle of the government of the day with an overwhelming majority, has the right to dictate that part of an adolescent's academic assessment shall include the extent to which he signs on to a participating democracy. Even for those pupils who are able to respond positively to such notions. What of the highly politicised for whom democracy is only one option. More significantly for my constituency, such a commitment has little or no meaning for the disaffected.

The very notion of a *National* Curriculum in England and Wales,' is authoritarian.

These proposals for education in Citizenship are about to become law. They then become statutory. Note the language of spin. The form of intervention in the curriculum is not described as a 'statutory requirement' of the government of the day. It's an *entitlement* of the children - to have imposed upon them the statutory requirements that they *shall* achieve *tightly defined learning outcomes.* By implication, if one opposes this proposal then presumably one is depriving the children concerned of their entitlement!

Ironically, the school that has probably done the most to explore the relationship between authority and democracy in the structuring and delivery of education to adolescents is Summerhill, founded by A.S. Neill. As I write, it is under threat of closure for non-compliance to the National Curriculum. Dramatically making her point about how schools are typically structured, Zoe Redhead, principal of Summerhill and daughter of, A.S. Neill, writes:

> Imagine a world where a child can tell you to fuck off not only with confidence, but with the joy of being an individual and sharing the revolution against the normal values of adult and child, that brings a warm shared smile or laughter between both of you.[28]

---

[28] Quoted. TES 28 May 99, p.5.

Nigel de Gruchy referring to children with emotional and behavioural problems says, '.... In 99% of the cases, the parents are the root of the problem.'[29] He might be right with regard to causation of the problem within the child but that the child goes into crisis within the school system is also largely influenced by how his disaffection is handled by the school. Anyone working with disaffected children will attest that there are teachers who seem to be effective with these kind of vulnerable pupils and those who invariably have problems and respond with rejection and ejection. The variation in response seems to centre upon how the teacher creates relationships and handles confrontation. This would suggest that it might be a question of personality and sense of security. As I noted elsewhere, an important informal measure of

---

[29] TES 28 May 99 p11. General Secretary, NASUWT.

teacher competence is their ability to handle challenging behaviour. Challenging behaviour puts huge professional and personal pressure upon the teacher.

Whilst I have argued that a programme might be on the wrong track that seems to set targets for emotional development as if they were skills to be learned and appears to regard an 'attitude' as though it was a cognitive skill that can be taught. The good news is that although the 'Citizenship' outcomes are prescribed, the curricular means are not. A 5% space in the curriculum has been created that might permit the application of psychoanalytic insights in a form of curriculum intervention that addresses these feeling deficits more appropriately.

CHAPTER FIVE

MANAGING RITA'S BEHAVIOUR

The major thrust of the Education service is that the disaffected child be taught to adapt to the service. There is huge reluctance to concede that the service ought to adapt to the needs of the child. Margaret Thatcher made school managers budget holders. The £2000+ plus per annum followed the child into the school as parents made what were supposed to be informed free choices when imposed catchment areas were abolished. Later, school comparative performance figures were compiled and published. The model is the market place. Dare I say the educational establishment is supposed to be competing in the market place for a clientele? The pupil as client!

The reality of the attitude of many staff to many disaffected pupils is very different. The condescension sometimes experienced trying to get past a National Health receptionist in a GP's surgery or when requesting NH service in a dental practice is very similar to that endured by difficult pupils. It is not only the insertion of the government block payment above the client and direct to the service provider that sets up the power relationship and the attitudes that flow from the power. The Education Service *is* upward referencing to government requirements not downward referencing to the pupil but other forces are in play. These teacher attitudes are part of the teacher's armoury of psychic defences as they wrestle with the deeply uncomfortable and try to preserve equilibrium in a highly unstable environment.

Additionally, as with for example, doctors and lawyers, there has been an interest in controlling access to information that can affect professional reputation and, increasingly, exposure to liability. Therefore there is a conspiracy of silence around faults in the system and the failures of personnel. But now there is a process of forced change. There is systematic external observation of teachers and publication of whole school results. As I have observed this might pressurise the school's pedagogic function and ironically inhibit its pastoral function because academic scores achieved are measured against national averages and then compared in published tables available in the school's local public library. Excluding troubled youngsters who might be disrupting class progress and therefore potentially damaging the school's results can appear to be a very attractive option. It could become increasingly attractive when teachers' pay is formally linked to performance.

As I write the first hospital league tables are being published. It will be very interesting to see how the defensive practices that will inevitably follow massage the results and affect patient care and to compare that out come with what is happening in education.

In the systems response to disaffected behaviour, I referred earlier to the irrationality of expecting different outcome behaviours from the same pupil responding in an unchanged environment. The only 'change' had been the formal repetition of admonitions. It was disregarding the same kind of admonitions that led to the crisis in the first place.

When the pupil has failed to respond and is under formal threat of exclusion there is usually a referral to a behaviour support service. The school's expectation is that this deviant pupil will be taught how to behave by learning strategies such as anger control. I have referred to the pupil-teacher relationship as structured by power. The pupil's defiance, in daring to challenge the status of the teacher, brings down upon himself reactionary pressures in support of the status of the teacher. The power system asserts its power.

The expectation is that the child will begin to manage his behaviour differently on the basis of fear of loss or desire for some future benefit of the education from which she might be excluded. This strategy had failed before, why will it succeed now? It is based upon seeking to change behaviour by an appeal to prudential considerations. This has its basis in an appeal to rationality. It is assuming that there is an effective pupil-teacher contract that is prudentially based. There is a great reluctance to ask why the pupil feels so apparently inappropriately angry, a reluctance to investigate the roots of the anger. It is my contention that the only way to achieve an effective pupil-teacher contract is first to establish an *affective* relationship. The immature adolescent relationships of the emotionally disturbed youngster are affectively bonded not prudentially bonded.

When the outreach teachers, as they are often called, try to befriend the pupil in his beleaguered state, as rapport is developed, they usually discover that behind the intransigence there are major personal issues. Many of these issues arise out of the failure of relationships in the family. The post Second World War families into which these children have been born are usually affectively bonded nuclear units. In the vast majority of cases the couplings that produced these children were based upon affective bonding flowing from sexual attraction. They were not prudentially arranged to protect or convey large family estates or wealth. Since the Second World War such bondings have proved to be highly unstable. It is estimated that one third to one half of the present school population at least are the product of single mothers or have been born into pairings that will not last the duration of the child's school education.[30]

It has been speculated that the economic dependency that prior to the Welfare State held

---

[30] Daily Telegraph article 20/6/99.

many families together has been weakened by the employment available to women and/or the economic support available from the State for one-parent families. This seems to be saying that one third to one half of school children are not being brought up jointly by both natural parents. It is estimated that both their natural parents will not raise more than 50% of children born to the present child bearing generation.

The preparedness of young sexually mature adolescents to tolerate the constraints of family life seems to be weakened by their perception of other options open to them in the form of hostels, bed sits and government subsidy. More than one sexually active disaffected 15 year old girl told me this term that it was her intention to get pregnant because then she could leave home and get a council house which she assumed the local council were obliged to give her. They claimed to have friends who had achieved just that. In June this year the government has announced the withdrawal of substantial support for single mothers and hostels as the only accommodation to be offered and then only in the direst of cases. Simultaneously it announced its determination to pursue adolescent fathers for maintenance payments for the children they sire.

These kinds of family situations produce enormous emotional strains upon adolescents and the relationships within the family. It is therefore no surprise that there are so many adolescents that do not know how to conduct a mature proactive relationship with a teacher or respond prudentially to the demands of authority. But ironically it is this very lack of close bonding in the family that is giving such an opportunity to the schools. It is my contention that these very same disaffected pupils are crying out for the anchor of an understanding relationship with an adult if the trust can be established upon which to build it. I maintain that the affective bond of respect and gratitude that can be established sets up the disaffected pupil to hear the voice of prudence, to learn the strategies of behaviour management. The outreach worker or teacher cannot demand that facilitating rapport. It is established by listening sympathetically. What they will hear will be very difficult to process. It will involve being the container for sometimes unbearable distress.

To flesh out the dilemmas facing these young people I am going to refer to some of my own cases working for Kent Behaviour Support Service. In that it is personal, it is anecdotal. However my weekly case conferences with nine other outreach workers confirm that my experience is broadly duplicated in theirs.

In my current case load of 40 disaffected or emotionally disturbed pupils aged 11 to 18 years only one is being reared by both his natural parents. Each of these pupils has been referred to me because their unacceptable classroom behaviour is likely to lead to their permanent exclusion from school or has already done so. I am tasked by the Behaviour Support Service to change that behaviour. In almost every case I have found it necessary to enable them to find help to change something in their wider lives first. It just does not work only to tell them that this is the reality of their lives and they must accept it and get on with it. So very often they are carrying such a burden of anger or resentment deriving from their emotional experiences that without support and change they just cannot create the trusting relationships with adults that would enable them to respond to the demands of the school.

I have changed the names, sometimes gender and other details, to protect anonymity in the following cases. Some of the details of their experiences are deeply disturbing. They are recounted solely to illustrate the sources of emotional damage that so much disaffected behaviour is expressing. Sadly these cases are not unusual. In fact every excluded pupil I have worked with has had a history of serious emotional damage. Every incident illustrated here that was a child protection issue has been reported and investigated. Mercifully I have very rarely been the recipient of initial disclosures.

These histories come from the families and the support agencies including the schools.

Susan aged 15 years was smoking cannabis in the lunch hour and being flagrantly disobedient in the classroom even inciting other children to disobedience. She hit crisis point by bringing vodka to school and getting so drunk that she had to be rushed to hospital and treated for alcohol poisoning. Whilst there the duty social worker refused to see her because the parent could not be contacted to give permission before she was discharged. She was not followed up. She then came to school with the lateral cuts on her wrists of another crisis. She demanded to be re-housed away from her mother in a foster situation or she would make another attempt upon her life. An extensive interview with the mother revealed incredible hostility between mother and daughter and absolutely no preparedness on either side to negotiate or compromise. Her mother claimed that Susan was completely out of control and looked to the school to do something. Susan claimed that her mother held her responsible for a £17000 legal bill and the resulting repossession of the home in the court action that gave the mother the current custody order. The divorce was very acrimonious and the original placement of the daughter with the father was overturned following a lengthy appeal. Her mother would not reveal where her natural father was living and Susan had not heard from him for over two years. Susan ran away and was missing for three nights and following her return was arrested drunk, disorderly and violent three nights later

When I put the girl back in touch with her father and the mother learned that he had come to visit her, the mother refused to let Susan back into the house. The parents of a friend gave her a bed and the Social Services finally opened her case and supported Susan in that temporary placement whilst the father negotiated with the police and Social Services that Susan could go to live with him in a different county.

During this time Susan had disclosed to me that she was having unprotected sex after smoking cannabis with a 27 year old who turned out to be a dealer using her as a conduit into the School. I arranged sexual counselling with a specialist clinic because the mother would not take her to a doctor. I referred her to Child and Adolescent Mental Health Services for an opinion on what appeared to be very serious depression but they declined to see her on the grounds that it was a family dispute and the social services were the appropriate supporting agency. At that time the Social Services had declined to become involved.

Prior to her move away she lived for a month with the friend's family who had housed her on the night her mother evicted her. In that month she was seeing her father at weekends. Her classroom behaviour improved greatly and her wildly erratic drinking stopped. Now she has been accepted into a new school in a different County close to her new home and is making progress. She is a bright girl and has recently written to say that she has got her head back into her studies and is expected to do well.

Ben is 15 and very disruptive. After his parent's divorce he went to live with his mother. Following a fall out and two weeks before Easter, he returned to live with his father. At Easter his mother came with an Easter egg and sitting with him in her car outside his father's house, begged him to return. He refused and by his own account was very sarcastic to her. She drove home and killed herself that night.

Jim is 15 and failing in school despite a good start. He is using cannabis in the lunchtime and before school when he can get it. He has sold most of his possessions, emptied a substantial savings account and is now stealing from his father. Whilst he was in hospital for a hip operation his mother visited him very regularly. She contracted a virulent virus, perhaps in the hospital, from which she died. His maternal grandmother has repeatedly accused him of being responsible for her daughter's death.

Angela is often violently confrontational with staff. She cannot tolerate her 'stepmother' who returns the dislike in double measure. The stepmother is older than her father and is having a very difficult menopause. Angela's father will not actually marry her in case she behaves like his first wife. She wants to be married. Angela's natural mother left when Angela was a baby and her father refuses to tell her anything about her including her whereabouts. He had promised to do so when she was 14 years old but changed his mind and has put it back until her 18th birthday. The father and daughter left their relatives, friends and home in the North to live with the stepmother after a courtship through a pen pal agency. Her father has largely abdicated and permits the stepmother to run the household and to apply boundaries to Angela's behaviour. He is imminently to be made redundant. Angela was discovered playing sexually with her young stepsister; she hides faeces in strange places and writes incredibly detailed accounts of her sexual requirements in letters to her boyfriend but leaves them around to be read.

Carol, aged 11, settles her arguments with her fists and is frequently violently confrontational in school. When she was younger her father made her watch as he inserted a coke bottle into the vaginas of her 11 and 13 year old sisters who were naked and tied up. He frequently abused the girls in a variety of ways. Her sisters are both failed in school, are unmarried, homeless and pregnant. The prosecution of the father failed. He went on to marry his ex-wife's sister. Carol's mother has had a series of breakdowns and is constantly depressed. She uses and supplies drugs to a local Health Farm. She recently disclosed to a neighbour that at 13 years old she had twin boys who were placed for adoption. Having recently traced them she visited one in his University digs. Allegedly he spoke of having sexual difficulties whereupon she had sex with him to help him out.

Amanda 18 is on Prozac and struggling with her A Levels that she should have passed with ease. She found her older sister having intercourse with her father. The father has left home but her sister has confided that she goes around to see him and still has sex with him. Her mother who knows about this is distraught.

The mother of Charley and Hayley was called to their two different Secondary schools on the same day. Hayley had been totally out of control. So had Charley. She had run from school having verbally abused the Headteacher. The girls had a history of such behaviour. Their older sister, Margaret sits at home with a phobia that forbids her to meet strangers. Their Father had adopted mother's other two children when they were infants. In their late teens they were told by mother's sisters that they were not his and taken to visit their natural father in prison. They were distraught. The girl turned from adoring her stepfather to accusing him of sexual abuse and takes to hard drugs. The Social services investigated and dismissed the case. The mother was diagnosed with cervical cancer. She is in remission. Her mother died of cancer in an hospice whilst being visited by Charley and Hayley. Father is diagnosed with a brain tumour. Disaffected daughter is found o/d with drugs. Mother rushes to the hospital forgetting a pan on the stove. The house burns down completely. There is no insurance. They lose everything. Well, not everything. Hayley rushes in and rescues her dog.

In every single case referred to me, I have found serious personal difficulties beneath the disruptive behaviour. These are amongst our most vulnerable pupils. The tendency is to expel them from school and exclude them from productive lives when they fail to respond to the demand to manage their behaviour. I have seen Headteachers exulting when they have excluded a pupil. The old term 'expelled' is much more revealing. The school, as a community, in the person of the Headteacher, has expelled, dare I say evacuated, that which it could not digest.

If we could interpret the gross discomfort and dislike engendered in ourselves when on the receiving end of the disaffection of these highly defended youngsters as introjecting their distress, would it help us to see it as their distress being felt inside ourselves? If we could see the Headteacher's action as countertransference would we evaluate it differently? Could we see it as evacuating that distress because it is uncomfortable even unbearable. If we find it unbearable, what is it doing to the pupil?

CHAPTER SIX

ILLUMINATING RITA

An essential component in the rehabilitation of Susan referred to in Chapter Five was a growth in her ability to understand from where the neediness was coming that made her so vulnerable. She gained an understanding of her mother's anger and rejection mirrored in her mother's own feeling of being rejected by her ex-husband. Susan began to see that her self-destructiveness and its roots in her low self-esteem related to her abandonment by her father and rejection by her mother. Importantly, she also saw its relatedness to the extremes of hostility her disaffection generated in many of her teachers.

This growth was partly achieved out of the one-to-one sessions with me. Much that was looked at in these sessions resonated for her with injunctions laid upon her in a less accessible way by her teachers and her parents speaking to her often in hostile tones driven by their anger and frustration. I would argue that my access to insights from psychoanalysis enabled me to see the rejection and anger that she attempted to provoke in me as functions of the transference and countertransference and as such a 'misrecognition' that failed in its purpose because I expected and recognised what was happening to me.

It is my argument that were these insights generally available to the teaching profession then far fewer disturbed pupils would be reactively excluded from their education. It was also possible to mitigate some of the harshness of the response from some of her teachers by sharing with them interpretations of her behaviour and their own response to it. Without their having a background of the relevant reading, this was an extremely delicate procedure. It was by no means universally welcome but I chose my collaborators carefully.

In the case of Susan I have shown how insights that flow from psychoanalysis helped her towards an understanding that she was displacing anger generated in her relation with her mother onto to her teachers. She is becoming alert to the situations in which that might happen and is better equipped to avoid, mitigate and ultimately control the consequences of that 'misrecognition'. What I am describing here is the transfer from psychoanalysis to Susan of insights that can illuminate the path to self-knowledge. But that 'self' knowledge' does not stop at the boundaries of the self. Susan needs to understand that the school's responses, whilst experienced as personal, are societal. That society interprets one of the requirements of self-knowledge to be the capacity of 'owning' one's behaviour. Whatever the personal psychoanalytic validity of an expression of disaffection, within the society of the school it will often be seen as provocatively disruptive, perceived as deviance and incur damaging sanctions. Successful adaptation to the expectations of the school will require that Susan adopt the school's interpretation of her disaffected behaviours as disruptive, therefore as deviant and therefore as deserving of the consequential sanction. In effect Susan will be required to accept the notion that she had effective choice, that she chose to be disruptive and that therefore she chose to receive the sanction. The school's view will be that a profound acceptance of personal social responsibility for ones behaviour is only possible when one ceases to cast oneself as a victim of consequences and recognises oneself as their author. The power structures within society, mediated through the school, will try to force acceptance of this 'recognition' upon Susan. She will be helped to ameliorate her anger if she can reach an understanding that 'society' as people in groups also seems to have profound anxieties not dissimilar to but perhaps even greater than her own; that such a society deploys violent defence mechanisms. Susan needs to understand that hostile intolerance of her nonconformity is an expression of group anxiety and her expulsion, a defensive response. Susan is beginning to see this.

Here I have focussed upon Susan's needs but it is also my proposition that society could manage its adolescents more effectively, more humanely, if these psychoanalytic insights were available within all schools. It also is my argument that psychoanalytic understanding has for far too long been medically monopolised and made effectively inaccessible to the majority of educators, therefore pupils, and therefore generation by generation, society at large. The transfer of the benefits of these insights to our troubled youngsters could flow from an informed teaching force. It could flow indirectly by better-informed responses to disaffection but it could also flow in a more direct ways if we could train psychoanalytically informed teachers to intervene directly in the social awareness of pupils. I do not see this intervention as acting as an information highways for some cognitively framed programme of Citizenship being currently promoted by the government. I see the intervention to be driven by *affects* from experiences gained within the teaching class as social group. More specifically, by a process that allows the pupils to identify themselves as a group with an agreed work focus and thereby simultaneously to grow into an identification of themselves as the engine of their own education not its passive beneficiary. This belief is founded upon insights from the phenomenology of group psychotherapy in the same way as that which I have described as flowing to the work with individuals from the phenomenology of individual psychotherapy.

Glassman and Wright describe as 'psychotherapy of the group' a model of group psychotherapy that might be effective with disaffected teenagers. They describe it as particularly suitable for patients with low motivation, low anxiety tolerance and personality disorders.[31]

Bion described the first basic principle of such a group as, 'the study of its own internal tensions in a real life situation, with a view to laying bare the influence of neurotic behaviour in producing frustration, waste of energy and unhappiness in a group.'[32]

The goal of such a model is to build a group culture that reinforces healthy functional behaviour. The assumption is that maladaptive behaviour has its roots in the individual's social system. In a group, the individual becomes aware of conflicts in personal relationships and their effect, as they

[31] Glassman, S.M. and Wright, T.L., 'In, with and of the group.' *Small Group Behaviour*, 1983, 14:pp.96-106
[32] Bion, W. R. 'The Leaderless Group Project,' *Bulletin of the Menninger Clinic*, 1946, vol. 10, 3; pp77-81

develop. There is not a one-on-one attempt to explore publicly with individuals the psychopathology that might lie at the root of their problems. The therapist's role is to be a peer model and thus equip the group with a role model to enable them to help each other. This peer group help will usually take the form of support for the development of healthy behaviours and discouragement of less adaptive behaviours.

To further this process, the therapist attempts to reduce the status and function difference between himself and members of the group. Initially this frustrates the group's need for dependency but it is done precisely in order to minimise the prolongation of the 'assumption of dependency' one of the subsets of group behaviours described by Bion as 'the basic assumptions.'

In describing the effects of the often unrecognised, irrational and powerful tensions that swirl in a group and using this understanding to a therapeutic end, Bion became a pioneer in a kind of social psychiatry. His resulting conceptualisation led him to a search for the causes of these powerful affects. In the surprising violence of the primitive underlying emotions he recognised a parallel with Klein's explanations of the rages of the infant. He began to see that the primitive emotions of the group were at their root primitive psychotic anxieties that might have their origins in the psychotic 'phantasies' of the infant's early object and part object relations proposed by Klein.

In trying to understand group behaviour and to use his understanding to a therapeutic end, Bion dealt with the here and now of presenting behaviours, albeit increasingly basing his personal understanding of what he saw upon Kleinian psychoanalytic thought. He did not seem to feel that the group was the place to publicly dissect the psychopathology of these manifestations of the unconscious. However he was very mindful that the therapist seek to be aware of what was happening at the unconscious level, understood projective identification and the effects of the resultant countertransference. The therapist's understanding was essential if he were to promote and not frustrate the therapy of the group by the group.

Memorably, Bion queried a dejected Eric Trist, a psychologist, and co-therapist. Referring to his emotional state after taking a Tavistock group, an emotion projected into him by the group, Bion asked, 'What does it make you want to do?' 'Give up,' was the reply.   'That is what the group members with the part of them that has no intention of changing, wants you to do. If you go along with them on this you will not help them. Always pay attention to what the group makes you feel.'[33]

The powerful level of unconscious resistance to change was an important factor in convincing Bion that his psychoanalytic approach to group dynamics was correct for it gave him an explanation in terms of powerful defence mechanisms against primitive psychotic anxiety.

J.D. Sutherland says that Bion believed that, 'by showing the group the ways in which it avoids its tasks through regressing to dependency, fight/flight, or pairing, it can become more work oriented and so

[33] E. Trist, 'Working with Bion in the 1940's: the group decade', in *Bion and Group Psychotherapy*, ed. M. Pine (London: RKP, 1992), p.30.

further the development of learning of all members.'[34] 'Work' here is being used in a dual sense. The process of behavioural change is the in-group work of the group but the group also was more effective if it was a work group with an external task or tasks. Bion realised that the in-group behaviours could illuminate the huge extent to which the group worked to avoid work or resisted learning from experience.

I find support for my theory that the 'Bion group' would be effective with disaffected adolescents in Sutherland's formulation of Bion's approach. Sutherland describes the approach as, 'seeing the problem of neurosis as a social one. How does the large organisation cope with the failures of its members to comply with its work task?' 'Failure'

[34] J.D. Sutherland, 'Bion Revisited: group dynamics and group psychotherapy', in *Bion and Group Psychotherapy, ed.* M. Pine (London: RKP. 1992), p.61.

here is a tendency negatively defined from the viewpoint of employer versus paid employee. I think that it is an assumption that the employee will see the problem as social in the sense of a shared problem rather than of straight conflict of economic interest narrowly defined where the employee does not naturally identify with the economic health of the employing corporate entity. Modern industrial relations seek to encourage the former view. If that position can be reached then critically Bion saw that the treatment of the problem has to be a problem for the group to solve within the group.

Yalom describes the intention of such a model as being to develop ' a group culture that is effective as a social system.' Here 'effective' is seen as to an end which is an agreed external group task or work focus and in relation to which the here and now processes of the group can be explored.

Yalom suggests that such a group is most effective when its existence as a group and its task is independent of the therapy but assisted by it. I believe that the focus of a group of disaffected adolescents, excluded from regular school because of maladaptive behaviour could be those healthy behaviours that assisted the group in its task of creating a milieu that supported the raising of the educational levels of the group; one that enabled the group to identify and commit to realistic educational goals. The educational goals would then become the external task of the group, the reason for its existence. I am not recommending this utilisation of explicitly therapeutic technique per se as the work of teachers but that of qualified therapists working with disaffected pupils already brought together in a specialist educational setting such as a Pupil Referral Unit for excluded pupils.

It would be important that this specialist educational setting be recognised as only a transitional space; that this supportive community be seen as a transitory community. That it not be allowed to become ' a closed society of neurotics that was acting against ... undertaking the more difficult task of establishing effective relationships in the 'normal society,' as Eric Trist reports of the denouement of a social club in a clinic.[35] The intention must be to reintegrate the individuals into a whole mainstream school environment.

Trist was writing of early post Second World War work just preceding Eysenk's seminal, 'The Effects of Psychotherapy'[36] which purported to demonstrate

[35] Trist, E., *Working with Bion in the 1940's: the group decade*, in Pine, M., (ed.) 'Bion and Group Psychotherapy', (1992) London: RKP. p. 34.

that psychotherapy had no proven benefit. These conclusions have been widely disseminated as proven but equally they have been widely challenged not the least in Roth and Fonagy's, 'What Works for Whom.'[37] In an award winning and wide ranging literature review published in 1997,[38] Hoag and Burlingame concluded, 'with the advent of meta-analytic techniques, child psychotherapy has been empirically demonstrated to be as effective as psychotherapy for adults' and further that meta-analysis of group psychotherapy with children and adolescents consistently demonstrated efficacy.

---

[36] Eysenck, H. J., The Effects of Psychotherapy: An Evaluation. *Journal of Consulting Psychology, 31, (1952), 355-324.*

[37] Roth, A. and Fonagy, Peter, *What Works for Whom? A critical review of psychotherapy research (London: Guildford Press, 1996).*

[38] Hoag, M.J. and Burlingame, G. M., Child and Adolescent Psychotherapy: A Narrative Review of Effectiveness and the Case for Meta-Analysis. *Journal of Child and Adolescent Group Therapy, Vol. 7(1997), No 2, pp. 51-68.*

This kind of success has been reported in recent therapeutic group work with imprisoned child sex offenders as measured by re-offending rates. Jack Straw,[39] referred to this success when, as Home Secretary, he was announcing the introduction of proposals to pre-emptively detain psychologically disordered patients previously regarded as having untreatable psychopathic personality disorders.

An awareness of these approaches could usefully underpin a teacher's work with disaffected pupils. For example, a teacher in a PTU trying to establish a cooperative learning consensus would never publicly pursue an investigation of the reasons for an individual disaffection. She would however be expecting the hostility that she would experience as the group resisted any articulation of the need for

---

[39] Jack Straw, House of Commons, 19th July, 1999.

personal growth and development. As she pursued the latter she would also expect to experience a very strong urge to give up. Forewarned she would understand that these powerful currents were natural to the psychodynamic of the group not an expression of the pupil's delinquency or her inadequacy.

If she felt able to persist, she would need to carefully downplay her role as leader thus throwing responsibility back upon the group. The group would then look for another leader. She could then help the pupils become aware of their need to be led rather than to be self directed. Eventually the opportunity would arise for the group to reflect upon the purpose for its existence that moment as a group and in that non teacher-directed mode.

That the voicing of just such a question could eventually be seen as an educational end in itself would be an ambitious but important goal. Eventually the group's original formal existence as a group to, say, advance understanding of mathematics in line with the legal requirements of the National Curriculum might emerge. Later some correlation between that and their own needs of a mathematical education to pursue their own goals might also emerge.

That many did not have such goals and resisted identification with the needs of those who could, would also emerge. That such pupils could not identify with the ostensible purposes of the teaching group would become apparent, as would their predisposition to 'disrupt' the group as it pursued goals with which they could not identify. This failure of identification - understood as such - could then become the focus of a reparative process within the group

Such a consensus would not be arrived at easily. As shown above, individuals in groups powerfully experience profound emotions. Teachers, who become deeply interested in these processes, will be fascinated to grasp Wilfred Bion's explication of Klein's work on the infant's primitive emotions re-merging in group interactions to which I have referred earlier. The developing adolescent will experience all kinds of emotional conflicts in the general frustration of trying to get a group to agree upon anything, still less to agree upon a common goal or to find the resolution to carry through an agreed course of action to its fruition. They will be strongly inclined to give up the attempt and to find someone to blame. That someone is usually the teacher for not assuming control and so fulfilling the pupils' assumption of dependence. The teacher steeped in the need to control and direct will experience the turmoil as even more discomforting. She must know that this is absolutely normal and highly educative for her pupils and even for herself.

Once achieved the consensus could be mobilised throughout the academic year to reinvigorate flagging motivation or to resist disruption. If consensus and identification fail to emerge or become disrupted it could also be 'progress.' Perhaps a radical rethink of what is perceived to constitute 'mathematics' is necessary or of its relevance as currently delivered in the curriculum of the group that is rejecting it. Perhaps even as delivered by that individual teacher to that group. As Bion discovered, these approaches are not only deeply challenging to the 'pupil.' They also challenge the status quo. That can be alarming for the 'management'. Bion was promoted sideways!

IN CONCLUSION

I must of course emphasise the very important distinction between a clinician applying a psychoanalytic technique in a specialist setting and a classroom teacher in working with the benefit of a psychoanalytic frame of reference. I regret that I have only been able to sketch-in an underpinning of my view of the applicability of psychoanalytic insights to education, to a forming of that frame of reference.

Again though there are great benefits to be had for the better-understood, disaffected pupil, it is also important to recognise that these insights could be of enormous benefit to the psychological health of the teacher. As the behaviour of pupils from dysfunctional homes proves, aggression, hostility and rejection are deeply damaging. Projected upon the teacher, they produce emotional turbulence and the urges for reciprocal antagonism. For the teacher to respond professionally not personally means swallowing those selfsame aggressive urges. Unaided, it is dreadfully stressful and often leads to depression and illness. Teachers deserve to be given the protection of a training that equips them to resist becoming helpless flotsam upon a stream of their own emotional turbulence - or that of their pupils.

Therefore, I believe that we owe it to *both* our staff and to our pupils to raise our level of awareness of the unconscious phenomena that shape challenging behaviours within our schools and that shape our responses to them. Only thereby can we make such behaviours intelligible then manageable. Uncomfortably we must start with ourselves. We have to resist our own 'instinctive' defensive responses to the unpleasantness of disaffected behaviours. Think of the surgeon encountering the stench of gangrene. He could run or he could operate.

This agenda implies a capacity to make oneself vulnerable, and to handle that experience in new and more emotionally taxing ways. Small wonder it encounters defences. The challenge is to contain this vulnerability. Not to control it, or project it. *To contain it.* It has to be acknowledged not as a hazard but as an occasion; the occasion for real work; the proof of being in touch and the means of keeping in touch.[40]

If we, as the teaching profession, can rise to this challenge, we will not continue to further abuse damaged pupils. We won't be aloofly delivering a

---

[40] David Armstrong, *ibid. - Writing in a different context of a similar process. Italics mine.*

curriculum to an address where they cannot live. We will be teaching effectively. We will see young people begin to be more in control of their less conflictive emerging selves. We will see them beginning to own their acquisition of education and skills.

Some of us will see ourselves surprised by the joy of rediscovering our own fulfilment in theirs.

Bibliography

Ainsworth, Margaret and Bowlby, John, 'An Ethological Approach to Personality Development', American *Psychologist,* 46 (1991), No 4.

Anderson, Robin and Dartington, Anna, eds., *Facing it Out: Clinical Perspectives on Adolescent Disturbance* (London, Tavistock, 1998)

Armstrong, David, *The Recovery of Meaning,* Tavistock Consultancy (URL, **www.human-nature.com**, 1997, last accessed July, 1999)

Armstrong, David, *Group Relations.* Tavistock Consultancy (URL, **www.human-nature.com**, 1998. last accessed, July, 1999)

Arnold, Magda B., ed., *The Nature of Emotion* (London, Penguin, 1968)

Audit Commission, *Misspent Youth '98* (London: Audit Commission Publications, 1998)

Aveline, Mark and Dryden, Windy, eds., *Group Therapy in Britain* (Milton Keynes, Open University Press, 1993)

Baum, Howell, *The Invisible Bureaucracy*, (Oxford, OUP, 1987)

Benedict, Ruth, *The Pattern of Culture* (London, RKP, 1961)

Berger, Peter and Luckmann, Thomas, *The Social Construction of Reality* (London, Peregrine, 1981)

Bernstein, Basil, *Class Codes and Control: Towards a theory of educational transmission* (London, RKP, 1971)

Bion, Wilfred, 'Group Dynamics – A Review', in *New Directions in Psychoanalysis,* ed. by Klein, M. (London: Tavistock Publications, 1955)

Bion, Wifred, *Experience in Groups* (London: Tavistock Publications, 1961)

Bion, Wilfred, *Attention and Interpretation* (London, Tavistock, 1970)

Bowlby, John, *Attachment and Loss.* Vols. 1-3 (New York, Basic Books, 1969 – 80)

Bloch, Sidney, *An Introduction to the Psychotherapies* (Oxford, OUP, 1986)

Cortazzi, Martin, *Narrative Analysis* (London,The Falmer Press, 1993)

Clarkson, Petruska and Pokorny, Michael, eds., *Handbook of Psychotherapy* (London, Routledge, 1994)

De Board, Robert, *The Psychoanalysis of Organisations,* (London, Tavistock, 1978)

Dewey, John, *Human Nature and Conduct* (New York, 1922)

DfEE, *Secondary School Performance Tables –
1998*, (London, The Stationery Office, 1999)

DFE, *The National Curriculum (*London, HMSO,
1995)

DfEE, *Social Inclusion: Pupil Support* (London,
The Stationery Office, 1999)

DfEE, *Excellence for all Children* (London, The
Stationery, Office, 1997)

Department of Health, *Working together under the
Children's Act. 1989 (*London, HMSO, 1991)

Dryden, Windy, ed., *Handbook of Counselling in
Britain (*London, Tavistock/Routledge, 1989)

Ekman, P. and Davidson, R. J., *The Nature of
Emotion (Oxford, OUP, 1994)*

Eysenk, H. J., 'The Effects of Psychoanalysis: an
Evaluation', *Journal of Consulting Psychology, 16
(1952)*

Ferenczi, Sandor, 'Psychoanalysis and Education', *International Journal of Psychoanalysis*, tran. by Michael Balint with 2 variants 30 (1949), 220-224.

Frosh, Stephen, *For and Against Psychoanalysis*, (London, Routledge, 1997)

Foucault, Michel, *The Order of Things* (New York, Random House, 1970)

Foulkes, S. H. and Anthony, E. J., *Group Psychotherapy* (London, Maresfield Library, 1984)

Freud, Sigmund, *Standard Edition of the Complete Psychological Works of Sigmund Freud*, tran. by James Strachey. 24 Vols. (London, Hogarth Press, 1953 -74)

Geleerd, Elisabeth, 'Evaluation of Melanie Klein's 'Narrative of a Child Analysis' *International Journal of Psycho-Analysis, (1962)*

Glassman, S. M. and Wright, T. L., 'In, with and of the group.' *Small Group Behaviour*, 14, 1983

Glover, Edward, *A Review of 'The Psycho-Analysis of Children,' by Melanie Klein.* London, IJPA, 14, (1933)

Nick Henwood, *Education Development Plan Consultation (*Maidstone, KCC, 1998)

Hoag, Matthew, and Burlingame, Gary, 'Child and Adolescent Group *Psychotherapy', Journal of Child and Adolescent Group Therapy,* 7, (1997) No. 2

Home Office, *Preventing Children Offending (*London, The Stationery Office, 1997)

House of Commons Select Committee on Education and Employment, *Disaffected Children (*London, HMSO, 1998)

Klein, Melanie, *The Psycho-Analysis of Children (*London, Hogarth Press, 1932)

Levi-Strauss, Claude, *The Savage Mind,* (London, Wiedenfield and Nicholson, 1962)

Lipgar, Robert M., *Beyond Bion's Experiences in Groups (URL* **www.sicap.it**, 1997, last accessed, June1999)

Lovell, K., *Educational Psychology and Children (*London, ULP, 1964)

Nietzsche, Friedrich, *Human All Too Human* (London, Penguin, 1994)

O'Neill, Robert, et al., *Functional Analysis of Problem Behaviour* (Sycamore, Il., Sycamore, Pub. Co., 1990)

Piaget, Jean and Inhelder, Barbel, *The Psychology of the Child,* trans. by Helen Weaver (London, RKP, 1969)

Pines, Malcolm ed., *Bion and Group Psychotherapy (*London, RKP, 1996)

Rapaport, David, *Emotions and Memory (*New York, IUP, 1950)

Rosenbaum, Max ed., *Group Psychotherapy and Group Function* (New York, Basic Books, 1963)

Sayers, Janet, *Mothering Psychoanalysis* (London, Penguin, 1991)

Seligman, Martin, The Effectiveness of Psychotherapy, *American Psychologist, 50 (1995) No 12*

Stanton, Martin, *Sandor Ferenczi* (London, Free Association Books, 1990)

Social Exclusion Unit, *Truancy and School Exclusion* (London, The Stationery Office, 1998)

Symington, Joan and Neville, *The Clinical Thinking of Wilfred Bion,* (London, Routledge, 1996)

Tanner, J. M., *Education and Physical Growth* (London: ULP, 1961)

Trudgill, Peter, *Sociolinguistics,* (London, Penguin, 1987)

Wells, H.G., *The Work, Wealth and Happiness of Mankind* (London: Heinemann 1932)

Yalom, Irvin, *Theory and Practice of Group Psychotherapy* (New York, Basic Books, 1970)

www.ingramcontent.com/pod-product-compliance
Lightning Source LLC
Chambersburg PA
CBHW062008280526
45787CB00005B/2018